Goss made just seven First World War models: Cenotaph, British six-inch incendiary shell, Bury St Edmunds German bomb, British tank, contact mine, Maldon German incendiary bomb and Russian shrapnel shell.

Goss and Souvenir Heraldic China

Lynda Pine

A Shire book

Published in 2005 by Shire Publications Ltd,
Cromwell House, Church Street, Princes Risborough,
Buckinghamshire HP27 9AA, UK.
(Website: www.shirebooks.co.uk)

Copyright © 2005 by Lynda Pine.
First published 2005.
Shire Album 440. ISBN 0 7478 0623 3.
Lynda Pine is hereby identified as the author of this work
in accordance with Section 77 of the Copyright, Designs
and Patents Act 1988.

British Library Cataloguing in Publication Data:
Pine, Lynda.
Goss and souvenir heraldic china. – (Shire album; 440)
1. Goss China Company Ltd
2. Souvenir china 3. Heraldic porcelain
4. Souvenir china – Collectors and collecting
5. Heraldic porcelain – Collectors and collecting
I. Title 738.2'8
ISBN 0 7478 0623 3.

Cover: *Arcadian camel, Carlton Flamborough fog siren building, Carlton Felix the Cat, Arcadian children in armchair, Corona tennis racquet, W. H. Goss miniature Trusty Servant beaker, Grafton singing cat, Carlton stick of Clacton rock, Arcadian petrol-pump attendant, W. H. Goss Rufus Stone and Carlton duck on green base.*

ACKNOWLEDGEMENT
Photography by Debbie Webb.

Printed in Malta by Gutenberg Press Limited, Gudja Road,
Tarxien PLA 19, Malta

Contents

Words printed in bold type in the text are explained in the glossary.

A model of a Tommy or First World War soldier driving an airfield tractor, as used on the Western Front, 80 mm long, Grafton.

What is souvenir heraldic china?

Ever since people started visiting the seaside in the early nineteenth century, resorts had offered souvenirs for visitors to take home as mementoes of their holiday. Such items were made of all sorts of materials – local stone, leather, wood, seashell or glass. They offered splendid opportunities for inexpensive collecting. Souvenirs bearing the local place-name were always popular, and when stalls and shops began stocking heraldic china with local **crests** the fashion for collecting was begun and spread all over Britain. In the 1880s the firm of W. H. Goss, acting on an idea of the owner's son, Adolphus, began supplying chosen agencies up and down the coast with small ivory **porcelain** shapes decorated with the local **coat of arms**. As the craze took off, Adolphus Goss travelled around Britain, selecting ancient pots in museums to copy in miniature in porcelain, and appointing a sole agency where they would be sold in each town. Appointed agents, while enjoying the exclusivity of their stock, found they could not get enough of the crested china to supply

A Brading (Isle of Wight) ewer with an enamel decoration of Henry, Duke of Warwick, 'King of the Isle of Wight', by Goss.

demand. Agencies included tearooms, lending libraries, chemists, railway station kiosks and newsagents, as well as fancy gift shops. Following the success of W. H. Goss, over a hundred and fifty other potteries copied their idea with their own versions of crested china.

The rule of souvenir china was that, wherever you went, you could only acquire a memento bearing the local coat of arms or a local view, so, for example, a Land's End crest could only be obtained from Land's End. This approach was followed by all the china manufacturers, who supplied their agencies only with the crest from their town or village. This is why there are so few pieces from remote villages in the mountains of Scotland or the Yorkshire dales – it was very difficult to get there to buy their crested china in the first place.

By this time the railways had developed sufficiently to allow people to take advantage of their 'wakes' and bank holidays, recently gifted by Queen Victoria, to travel further than had previously been possible. Thousands of workers deserted the towns as they invaded the coast and seaside boarding houses. Subsequently, the invention of the motor car enabled those who could afford one an even greater chance to travel wherever they chose. Open-topped charabancs could be hired for parties of up to twenty passengers at a time. As others travelled by bicycle, coach and even paddle steamer, the trend was for people to become more inquisitive and acquisitive.

Nearly all crested china was made in the Potteries in North Staffordshire. This area had developed over the centuries because of the local supplies of clay, flint, coal and water power. The potting industry had suffered a big depression in the second half of the nineteenth century and the craze for souvenirs revitalised many firms, who switched production from their normal tableware and sanitary ware to miniature ornamentals.

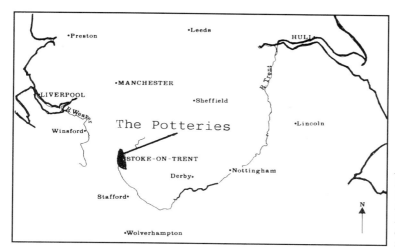

A map of England showing the location of the Staffordshire Potteries, where crested china was made.

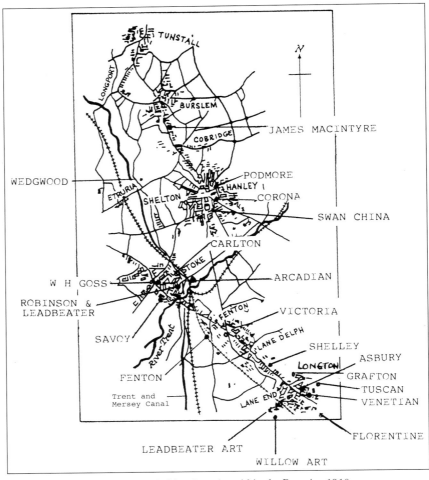

A map showing the main crested china factories within the Potteries, 1910.

At the centre of the Potteries was Stoke-on-Trent, where the Goss **pottery** was sited. To the north were Hanley, Shelton, Etruria, Cobridge, Burslem, Longport and Tunstall. To the south lay Fenton, Lane Delph, Lane End and Longton. Virtually all the other potteries which attempted to produce crested ware were located within this area. There were a few exceptions, such as some Irish and Scottish firms, and Worcester. Apart from W. H. Goss, the main manufacturers of crested china were Savoy, Carlton, Grafton, Shelley, Willow Art and Arcadian, the last being the most prolific after Goss. The Irish firms were Belleek, Arklow, Colleen and Shamrock China, and Scottish makers included Nautilus, Celtic Porcelain and Lochinvar.

A close-up of the Goss crest of Gloucestershire County Council.

Decorations on heraldic china

Heraldry developed throughout Europe from 1130 onwards so that soldiers in armour could identify one another in battle. The heraldic signs adopted were jealously guarded and eventually all nobility had their own shields. Each part of the design of a heraldic device has meaning and its own terminology; the language is Norman French.

Cities, towns and boroughs throughout Britain eventually had their arms to display on public buildings and official writing paper, usually with Latin mottoes on a scroll underneath. It was these that the Goss factory, and the firms which followed, reproduced exactly on souvenir china. These colourful shields were of great interest and were ideal for decorating the mementoes sought by visitors to the town. Most coats of arms had a crest immediately above the shield, such as the pine tree above the Bournemouth arms; some towns, such as Southampton, had 'supporters' at

A close-up of the Goss crest of Stroud.

A close-up of the Goss picture seal of Linslade Urban District Council.

the sides of their shield, so adding variation. Additions to an agent's stock of town or city arms included pieces inscribed 'See of ...', or mentioning a local abbey or family, as well as pieces decorated with a transfer of a local scene.

Before the advent of the picture postcard in about 1901 transfer scenes showing a view of the town or scenery, in colour or plain black, red, green, blue or, more usually, brown, featured on many souvenir ware pieces, as an alternative to a coat of arms. Sprays of flowers or lucky white heather with a scroll inscribed 'A present from ...' or lucky black cats painted in a variety of poses with 'Good luck from ...' made a desirable souvenir. These were inspired by the original drawings of W. H. Hosband in the early 1920s. Further variations include Masonic symbols such as the square and compass, regimental badges (from 1914 onwards), naval badges, christening initials made of forget-me-nots, and various designs of flora and fauna. Also produced on Goss and crested china were school and university arms, overseas crests, verses, legends and mottoes with illuminated lettering, exhibition arms and commemoratives. Some of the more intricate arms are those of the various nobility and royalty.

A Wilton Felix transfer 'From Porthcawl'. On the reverse is printed 'Pathe presents in every boys preview'.

The manufacturing process

Potting was an art, and each pottery's porcelain had its own distinctive quality and feel. The **parian** body that was used for crested china had been invented only around 1870–1 by both Minton and Copeland. Unglazed, it had a look and feel of **biscuit** and was used for busts and figurines. It was also ideal for making miniature **hollow ware**, which was then **glazed**. The manufacturing process of crested china was very similar from one pottery to another.

The raw materials were brought in, often on the Trent & Mersey Canal, and prepared either on site or at local grinding mills. Felspar, white glass, selenite, flints, white sand, potash and Cornish **kaolin** were the main ingredients of liquid parian. Each shape was made in at least two pieces from **moulds**. Liquid parian or **slip** was poured into the mould and after about ten minutes poured out again, leaving a thin lining of parian called a cast. Moulds had a short life and continually had to be remade to keep the sharpness of the design. The moulds were always about 25 per cent larger than the eventual pieces because parian contracted during the drying out and **firing** stages, and the moulds, which were made of plaster of Paris, absorbed so much water. Casts had to stay in the moulds for a further half hour, drying in front of a stove. This stage was called 'casting'.

When the mould was opened up, the contents had to be joined together to make a whole shape. The repairer, who worked in the 'green house', had to **fettle** the edges to make sure there was an exact fusion. This was a particularly skilled job, especially with composite shapes that needed parts from several moulds. It was at this stage, while pieces were damp, that any impressed marks were applied. The **green ware**, as it was known, stayed in the green house for up to a week to dry out thoroughly and have any blemishes removed.

Now the improved green ware was ready for the first biscuit firing. Pieces were placed in **saggars** in the room next to the **kiln** or oven, often called the placing room or saggar house. Placers embedded the items in ground flint in layers in the saggars, which were about 50 cm long, and then carried them into the oven, where they stacked them like hat boxes, one on top of the other, the one above acting as a lid for the one below. After the first firing, what had gone in as green ware came out of the oven as biscuit ware.

The oven walls were 60 cm thick, usually round and made of the hardest firebrick. There were fire openings around the base of the oven with **flues** underneath to spread the heat. The main flame went up the middle, where empty saggars with no bases were stacked, to the chimney. Space was valuable, so every possible bit of the chimney was loaded with full saggars of ware.

An external view of a typical bottle oven.

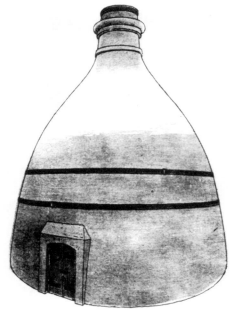

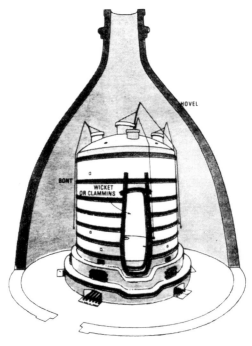

Above: *A cross-section showing the inner oven within the hovel, or outer shell of brickwork.*

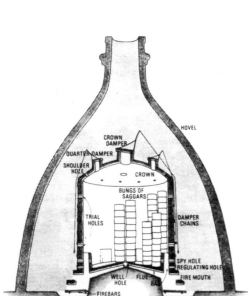

A cross-section of an oven.

Sometimes firing dust got into the glaze of the finished product when the saggars splintered during firing. An average oven would take about two thousand saggars. The placers had to climb ladders to position the upper ones, known as horses and circular in shape so that they rested securely against the oval bungs (stacks of saggars).

No two ovens behaved in exactly the same way and the **fireman** knew his own oven best. The fires were lit well beforehand as the ovens took a long time to heat up, so the men were still stacking as the fires were burning. The fireman would be up all night continually stoking the eight or so fires around the oven base. It would take about fifty hours to fire and another three or four days to cool. On average 22 tons of coal were used for each firing of an oven so that a temperature of between 1000°C and 1200°C was reached. The firemen endured intense heat. A full oven regularly fired kept everyone else employed. When the firing was over, the fires were drawn and the bricked-up door or **clammins** was broken down. Workers entered to remove the saggars carefully one by one, carrying them away on **wareboards** on one shoulder to the biscuit warehouse. Unscrupulous bosses would force workers to go into the ovens before they had properly cooled down; the men had to wrap wet towels around their heads under their caps to cope with the intense heat.

At the biscuit warehouse women emptied the ware out of the saggars and brushed away the ground flint. Any spoiled pieces were sent to the spoil heap. It was at this stage that ware was stamped with a printed factory mark. Any defects in the china were sanded down by hand (by machine after 1903 in some factories). The ware was then glazed. This process was called **dipping** and was carried out in the dipping house. The biscuit ware was dipped individually into vats of cold glaze, which resembled thin cream. Each item was hooked with wire and quickly inserted and withdrawn, being flicked in a circular wrist action to spread the glaze evenly before it could congeal. Not every item was glazed – unglazed items bypassed the dipping house. When the glazed pieces were dry they were sent to **glost kilns** for firing. This took between sixteen and twenty-four hours, with the ovens reaching a temperature of about 1000°C and burning 5 tons of coal per firing. Extra care was taken and the saggars used for this stage were glazed inside. Pieces inside them were kept apart by **props** or **cones** made of silica sand and shaped in triangles, which were placed under and above the pieces to keep them apart. The three points where the props held them apart can still be seen under some pieces, with fragments of sand fused to the base.

After glazing the shapes were sorted into bins in the sorting house. Pieces of the same shape were kept together until selected to fulfil orders.

In the **printing** shop the printer put the copper plate engraved with the coat of arms or other pattern on the stove to heat. Black ink (it was usually black) and oil were added with a flexible knife to the plate before the excess ink was scraped off. The plate was then polished with a pad to leave the colour only in the interstices of the engraved pattern. Tissue was pressed on and the plate was rolled in a press. The engraving was then carefully peeled off the copper and given to the cutter, who would cut off the excess paper and then pass the transfer to the transferrer. She would apply the transfer to the correct place on the piece by hand. Another lady would rub soap on top until the transfer was fixed. Not all shapes had a smooth surface and the transfer had to fill in the intricacies of the shape. It was then left for a day before the tissue was washed off, which in turn fixed the transfer.

Next, the pieces went to the enamelling house, where paintresses sat in rows with a framed sample coat of arms above them to copy. The outline of the design was already on the china from the transfer, so all the paintresses had to do was colour it in with **enamels** applied with a paintbrush.

Gilders painted the rims of items that needed a gold finish. In the **gilding** house gilders sat at revolving wheels set in motion by hand and held a steady brush to the rim of the piece in the centre of the wheel. After gilding wares were fired in small **muffle kilns**. This firing could take between five and nine hours, the temperature reaching 700°C to 800°C, and using up to a ton of coal per firing. Pieces were placed apart inside the oven on perforated iron slabs or **bats**, which acted as shelves.

The underside of a Carlton model and an Arcadian model. Some of these artefacts were numbered by their factories. Note the paintress's marks and the agent's mark on the Shrewsbury ewer (left).

The pottery town of Longton during the day, 1906.

The quantity of coal used in all the bottle ovens in the Potteries, night after night, year after year, caused a continual black smog in the air. The Clean Air Act of 1960 rendered the bottle ovens obsolete overnight, with firms changing to modern gas and electric kilns. Most of the bottle ovens were demolished, making way for new developments and roads. There are now preservation orders on the few bottle ovens that survive. Portmeirion, the pottery that now stands on the site of the Goss factory, have rebuilt the Goss ovens, which had been allowed to fall into disrepair, and the Gladstone **potbanks** at Longton have been wonderfully restored and are open as a museum.

The pottery town of Stoke during the evening.

The packing area of the Goss factory c.1920.

Goss china

The firm of W. H. Goss

From 1858 William Henry Goss ran his small pottery in St John Street, Stoke-on-Trent, next to the premises of his former employer, Copeland China. His early ware (First Period) consisted of busts, figurines and ornamental shapes made in parian, mainly unglazed, with some enamel hand-colouring, especially turquoise and gold. He had important and influential friends in the arts world and received early recognition for his pieces, which resembled those he had produced for his former friend, Alderman Copeland. These classical pieces were popular with the wealthy middle classes, who did not quite aspire to owning busts and figurines of real marble, but they were not produced in vast numbers and were time-consuming to make. The first political busts sold were of Lord Palmerston, whose second term of office as Prime Minister was from 1859 to 1865. These were marked 'Copyright' and, when the porcelain was still damp, incised with Goss's signature. Busts were Goss's forte; his close friend, Llewellyn Jewitt, reviewing his bust of Gladstone, wrote in *The Reliquary*:

> It conveys to the eye a far more truthful speaking and eminently pleasing likeness of the great statesman, than has ever yet been produced either by painting, engraving or sculpture. It is a splendid and faultless work of art and one that will well sustain Mr. Goss's reputation as the leading portrait bust producer of the age.

Goss exhibited at the Great International Exhibition of 1862 and won an important medal for his parian display. It was complimented in Cassell's *Illustrated London News* of 15th November 1862: 'The perfection of art manufacture seems certainly to have been reached.' 'Ivory porcelain' was the term used for his own particularly fine type of parian. Goss spent hours experimenting in his workshops, using his knowledge of chemistry to perfect his parian. He kept his recipes secret, although he was famously betrayed when his best twelve men left him for Belleek in Ireland. When **terracotta** suddenly became fashionable between 1866 and 1867 Goss attempted to work in that type of reddish brown **earthenware**, producing wine bottles, jardinieres, tobacco jars and a variety of vessels in the Greek and Roman styles, but this production lasted only two years. Goss was one of the few firms to mark its wares.

Three W. H. Goss parian busts: Southey, Granville and W. H. Goss himself.

A W. H. Goss tea plate with an enamel decoration of 'Robin Hood's Last Shot'.

It was their keen shared interest in history, archaeology and heraldry that led William and his son Adolphus to make models of historic objects found in museums. Adolphus had the idea of applying the coats of arms of schools and universities as transfers on the pieces, which were then sold at the school or college.

Being a natural businessman, he made the scheme a success. Realising he had a saleable commodity, Adolphus began applying the coats of arms of towns and the nobility, a move that was to transform the profile of the company. Instead of each piece being produced individually, moulds were made to accommodate several pieces at a time, to be used successively, in order to supply the increasing demand and keep costs down. In 1883 Adolphus wrote to his brother Godfrey in the United States, 'We are still so busy that I cannot go out after orders as we could not execute any more.' As sales manager and artistic director, his original intention had been to supply only matching crests, so, for example, a Reading urn had a Reading crest, but the agents found this too limiting and after 1883 they were allowed to order any

A W. H. Goss beaker with black transfers of 'Town Hall, Portsmouth' and on the other side 'St. Thomas' Church, Portsmouth'.

'Dorothy Vernon's Porridge Pot', with the arms of the Duke of Fife and 'Braemar', by W. H. Goss and an urn with the arms of Lord Kitchener, also by Goss.

shape they wanted from stock as long as it bore the coat of arms of their town. After 1885 Adolphus's son Dick began to help him, touring the country, securing agencies and choosing new subjects for modelling. Eventually most areas of Great Britain were represented. Adolphus covered England, Wales and the Isle of Man; Dick looked after Scotland, Cornwall and the Channel Islands. By 1900 they had secured 481 agencies in Britain and began to secure agencies overseas.

Apart from his roles as commercial traveller and sales manager, Adolphus was also the company's chief designer and artistic director and helped train

This W. H. Goss sales photograph with numbered shapes and models was sent to all the agencies, c.1928.

A photograph from the beginning of the twentieth century of London Road, St Leonards-on-Sea, with the Goss agency on the left.

the paintresses. He irritated his father by calling himself 'Goss Boss', and indeed the firm's workers began to look upon him as such. William's fury was such that, on his death in 1906, he bequeathed the pottery to his other sons while Adolphus was left only money. The result was that Victor and Huntley Goss were so short of money after paying Adolphus off that the firm never recovered financially. Without the two most skilled members of the family, it had to contend with effective competition from other firms and was further damaged by Victor's untimely death from a riding accident in 1913. Huntley was neither a skilled artist nor a good businessman; the firm, led by him and his artistic sons Noel and John, struggled to survive when the First World War began in 1914 and was further damaged when many of the male staff joined the armed services. The numerous debts owed by the overseas agencies went largely unpaid and this helped bring about the Goss pottery's demise.

The factory was eventually sold in 1929 to Goss's rival, Harold Taylor Robinson, the owner of Arcadian and Willow Art and many other factories. However, the mark of Goss (usually 'Goss England') was used for another ten years on a variety of ware, including some colourful pieces such as ladies and cottage pottery.

Goss china ware

One of Adolphus's best ideas was to produce coloured models of famous buildings such as Shakespeare's house at Stratford-upon-Avon. He began these in 1893 and they became a very popular range. They did not bear coats of arms, nor did the series of brown crosses and some other unglazed monuments. All the coloured examples of Goss are perfectly modelled and faithfully hand-painted to reproduce exactly the originals from which they were copied.

Apart from the cottages, the more expensive lines were the fonts, crosses, shoes, white glazed buildings and models made for the League of Goss Collectors. The fonts include those from Hereford Cathedral and St Martin's church, Canterbury, and most have variations in both white and brown uncrested, unglazed parian, as well as in white glazed parian, usually with a matching crest. The Winchester font is a huge, heavy, square piece in black or white while the Southwell Cathedral font is delicate and paper-thin.

The Goss crosses are nearly all pre-1900 and, like the fonts, were produced in white or brown, glazed or unglazed, but without crests. The chosen originals were usually from remote spots in distant parts of Scotland or other mountainous regions, so the most ardent Goss collectors were severely tested. The inaccessibility of these locations probably accounts for the rarity of the pieces now. They were also somewhat expensive at the time, costing between a shilling and one shilling and sixpence each. The brown versions often have tinges of green and shadings of brown to simulate moss and age. One particularly magnificent example is the St Martin's cross, Iona, which was copied in stone in 1906 to mark the grave of William Goss in Hartshill cemetery, Stoke-on-Trent.

The League models were made for the members of the League of Goss Collectors, formed in 1904. On joining the League members received a free Portland Vase; after two years they received the Pilgrim's Costrel; after four the Staffordshire Tyg; and after six the King's Newton Anglo-Saxon Cinerary Urn. All the League models were decorated with the circular League arms, which featured the Goss family crest with the Latin inscription *Semper fidelis*, meaning 'Forever faithful'. A further fifteen beautifully crafted models represented the years after the war, 1918–32, but they were expensive and came with the 'international' version of the design.

Goss pieces often came in series, giving the collector the objective of collecting all of the range. One series consisted of shoes and one of the earliest models was the Princess Victoria's First Shoe; after Queen Victoria's death in 1901 it was reworked on the base 'the late Queen'. William Goss gave the Queen an early model. In a letter dated 2nd January 1893 he discusses the shoe he gave to Queen Victoria through a lady friend, Mrs

Samuel Carter-Hall. Victoria owned several pieces of Goss, which can still be seen at Osborne House, Isle of Wight.

Three Goss lighthouses: Portland, Longships off Land's End, and Blackgang Tower, Isle of Wight.

The lighthouse series is interesting in that nearly all the originals are still standing and can be visited today. The likeness is excellent. Some, like the Portland and Beachy Head pieces, have a coloured band that was issued in brown, red or black, possibly because the original lighthouses changed their colours.

During the Second Period Goss produced named models, which cover a wide range of models, from delicate to heavy, pretty to unusual, including baskets (one round wicker fish basket is called a 'craisie'), barrels, bricks, goblets, pitchers, water coolers, braziers, jacks, salt lumps, pipes, lamps and measures. There is even a chantry, a canoe, various shells and a Cornish pasty! A special line was the numbered Egyptian models including a pyramid and a canopic jar with Anubis head. Collectors liked to obtain an example of each and travelled for miles in their quest for an elusive piece. These crested artefacts, plus a range of domestic ware, sold from about sixpence each. There are over four hundred named models and over a hundred and forty shapes that are not named, and which can be either ornamental or useful. The more expensive and therefore scarcer models were beyond many collectors' price range at the time. Pieces from the Third Period, after the factory was sold, comprise highly glazed, colourful ware as well as miniature buildings, Toby jugs, crinoline ladies and motto ware.

Other crested china potteries

Arcadian china and Harold Taylor Robinson

After 1929 Goss china continued to be produced by Harold Taylor Robinson, who already owned the Arcadian China Works and many others, including Willow Art, which he bought in 1925 when it was virtually bankrupt. Arcadian china was made by Arkinstall & Son Ltd at the Arcadian works, Stoke-on-Trent, on a site now under the main road through the Potteries, situated by the Queensway interchange and Church Street, the factory being long since gone.

Arcadian was by far the largest manufacturer of crested souvenir ware after Goss. More Arcadian crested china was produced than any other make, all because of the energy and ambition of one man, Harold Taylor Robinson. He began in 1899 as a traveller for Wiltshaw & Robinson (who made Carlton china) when only twenty-two years old and had accumulated enough capital (£1500) to start up on his own four years later, trading as Arkinstall & Son Ltd. Whereas other potteries produced crested china as a sideline, this firm was possibly the only one to be set up to manufacture crested china and nothing else. Robinson

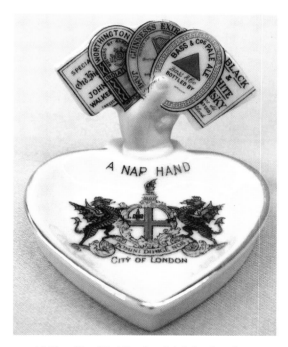

'A Nap Hand' holding beer labels by Arcadian.

*A British
cavalry officer
and Russian
Cossack, both
on horseback
and both by
Arcadian.*

began to increase his empire by taking over other potteries, for example Robinson & Leadbeater in 1910. He capitalised on the First World War by copying every type of battleship, tank, bomb and aeroplane, and also produced figures of soldiers (Tommies), including items of their kit. The First World War models were made as quickly as possible to supply demand. He showed his business acumen by providing the public with military souvenirs based on newspaper reports and photographs almost as soon as they appeared in print. He registered his models so that he could collect the dues from other manufacturers who followed him. The Arcadian First World War range is the largest and includes certain models not made by any other manufacturer, such as the anti-aircraft shell. His range of war memorials made in the first few years after the war is also the most extensive. Robinson then took over Swan China, Coronet and Cauldron. He continued to use the Goss mark and produced his own style of Goss ware, usually marked 'Goss England'.

Arcadian exhibited at the British Industries Fair of 1920 and the British Empire Exhibition at Wembley, 1924–5. By the 1920s the company was providing stock for over ten thousand agencies all over Great Britain and abroad. It continued making china until

Arcadian's British soldier standing to attention, with the arms of Wool.

'Petrol Sir': a saluting Arcadian petrol-pump attendant, with the arms of Havant.

at least 1933. Whereas Goss had had only one outlet in each town or city, Arcadian ware was sold in every conceivable retail outlet – seaside kiosks, piers, bazaars, cafes, stationers, post offices, chemists, lending libraries – as well as china shops. It was one of the few firms to make use of publicity. One of its last advertisements was in the *Daily Mail* of 22nd May 1928:

> Arcadian Arms China can be obtained from over 10,000 Retail Fancy Goods Stores in practically every town and village in Great Britain, decorated in correct colours and local Coat-of-Arms. If not already collecting Arcadian Arms China, START AT ONCE! It is a fascinating hobby. The collection of Arcadian Arms China creates an added interest and preserves pleasant recollections of a holiday. Friends will appreciate nothing better than a gift of Arcadian Arms China on your return.

An Arcadian alarm clock set for 6 o'clock, inscribed 'Many are called but few get up'.

Arcadian registered series number 13, Black Cat Radio Operator.

One of Arcadian's ranges was the Black Boys, who were featured in a series of busy poses, in a bath or eating a melon, up a tree or in the shower, all with a silly grin. These were all made after 1925 and so had a relatively short shelf life. There were also appealing children with blonde hair and rosy cheeks sitting in cosy armchairs, on a log or in the bath.

Another of Robinson's popular themes was items made for the 'luck' market. These included pieces (often hat boxes, armchairs or ashtrays) decorated with lucky white heather and the accompanying motto 'A present from ...' followed by the place name, and others decorated with lucky black cats, and sometimes with swastikas, which had traditionally been used as symbols of good luck before being adopted by Hitler and the National Socialist party.

In another rare piece of advertising, Arcadian published in 1925 a catalogue of their stock. The only items featured in colour were the twenty-four miniature 'black cat' pieces, registered in 1924. Most of these sold for two shillings each, the more intricate ones for half a crown. These sporting black cats were riding a sledge, peering out of a well, sitting on a horseshoe, paddling a canoe or sailing a yacht.

Two of Arcadian's Black Boy series: 'A little Study in Black and Fright', with the boy startled to see a spider crawling up his bedclothes, and 'A Black Bird from .... Cheddar', with a black head popping out of an egg.

In all his potteries Robinson produced intricate buildings (especially the Willow Art models). He favoured nostalgic, domestic objects such as a lace iron and a bed pan, a kitchen range with its mantel cloth and cooking pot on the fire, bellows and petrol cans – providing the modern collector with an insight into a way of life that has long since disappeared.

The Robinson empire swallowed up most of the smaller potteries, over twenty in all, although Carlton managed to stay independently owned. Robinson became the largest employer in north Staffordshire and dominated the production of heraldic ware. He was a director of thirty-two companies and had visions of forming an amalgamation of all his companies, which included firms to provide fuel and clay. He was ahead of his time. However, even a businessman of his stature was not immune to the economic Depression of the 1930s. In 1932 Robinson informed his bankruptcy hearing that he had been assured by a respectable accountant that if outside events had not overtaken him he would have been a millionaire. He was quoted in *The Pottery Gazette* as saying at the hearing:

> When I saw the Depression was developing to the extent it was, I left my country house and came to live practically next door to the works and I have been working fifty weeks out of fifty-two to try to circumvent the terrible effects of that Depression. When you get down to basic facts you will realise that as the largest potter in north Staffordshire, I have been the largest victim.

He managed to continue trading until the late 1930s, when he slipped quietly from the business scene after a long and colourful career.

Willow Art

Another prolific china factory was Willow Art, situated in Longton between Garden Road, Willow Row and Trentham Road. It made a good-quality porcelain with a slightly more greyish tinge than Arcadian's, which was more creamy white. It is more famous for its monuments and cottages but produced a good range of most of the popular themes, such as animals, the First World War, transport and nostalgic domestic items such as miniature cheese dishes, alarm clocks and miniature teapots. As with most of the factories, many Willow Art pieces are unmarked but can be distinguished by their hand-painted stock numbers and, in some cases, the agent's name and address in a rectangular box on the base.

Shelley china

The Shelley family began producing crested china after 1903. Early pieces were marked 'Foley'; most items were numbered, with the exception of tableware. After 1910 the trade name was changed to Shelley, possibly to avoid confusion with other Foley china. Shelley was very much in competition with W. H. Goss for the trade in artefacts, and its pieces were just as carefully made and with beautifully painted crests, with the distinctive yellowish glaze. The Shelley factory is still standing in Longton, near the junction of Hollings Street and Brocksford Street.

A lantern, comical pup and upright piano by Shelley.

The Laxey Wheel, Isle of Man, by Carlton.

Carlton

Most factories had variations to the factory mark used on their wares and Carlton was no exception, with eight marks. In 1902, after they had fulfilled most of their orders for the coronation of Edward VII and Queen Alexandra, the firm advertised their latest speciality, 'Carlton Heraldic China'. The quality of Carlton can vary but most of the heraldic ware is very fine and of superior quality. The firm was best known for its battleships, buildings (nearly all white glazed) and its vast range of historical, traditional and national ware. Its animals included

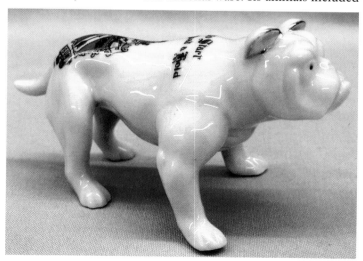

A fierce bulldog by Carlton, inscribed 'Slow to start but what a hold!'

Above: *Carlton's John Bull with bulldog, a truly patriotic piece!*

some original shapes, notably an ambitious pair of stags with antlers and the series of birds on a green base. Carlton is well represented with its First World War models. It was the only firm to model a munitions worker holding shells, labelled 'Doing her bit' and 'Shells and more shells', and Bruce Bairnsfather's comical cartoon figure Old Bill, with the caption 'Yours to a cinder'. Carlton survived until 1988 but no crested china was made after 1930. The pottery building still stands in Copeland Street, Stoke-on-Trent.

Savoy

Savoy china (Birks, Rawlins & Company) was made at the Vine pottery in Stoke-on-Trent, situated between Fletcher Road and Roden Street, over the road from the house William Goss lived in at one time and a few roads away from the Goss pottery. Savoy followed other potbanks in producing crested china from about 1910. The firm found its trade increased after the war and advertised in *The Pottery Gazette* for a couple of years. Savoy's First World War pieces are

A Savoy pierced puzzle jug with a rhyme on the back: 'How to drink and not to spill, to try the utmost of thy skill'.

A miniature nine-piece teaset by Savoy, with the arms of Harrow.

outstanding, especially the biplanes and battleships. Savoy china has a slightly gritty texture and the mouldings are highly detailed and much more unusual than those of most other manufacturers. It also sold a large range of First World War battle commemoratives with detailed inscriptions, which are still surprisingly clear to read. These are usually on mundane vases but do appear on busts and war models. Savoy also had a stand at the British Empire Exhibition but a few years later succumbed to the Depression and merged with Carlton in 1932.

Grafton

Of the one hundred and fifty other manufacturers, Grafton (Alfred B. Jones & Sons) china is the most notable, with its translucent glaze and delicate modelling. This firm hand-painted the stock number on the base of its crested ware, which was produced from 1900. Grafton ware was termed 'badge ware' and its colour transfers 'view ware'. After 1906 it promoted 'transparent ivory arms ware', making more interesting shapes than simple named models and domestic ware. Grafton started to sell First World War themed china towards the end of the war, and had displays at all the national exhibitions. Its most notable models were the 'Bomb Thrower' and 'Over the Top', with a soldier with rifle climbing over a mound. It also produced animals with glass eyes held in place by wire. The firm survived the Depression and made crest ware until 1933, before switching production to tableware. The factory is still in Longton, between Marlborough Road and Belsay Close.

The German competition

The German souvenir-ware industry was supplying European countries long before Adolphus Goss had led the way in England. The German potteries produced cups, saucers, plates, teapots, jugs and bowls with scenes of localities; the earlier ones were brown or black transfers but later scenes were hand-coloured. Ribbon plates with reticulated rims threaded with ribbon were particularly prized. From about 1860 onwards firms such as P. Donarth of Bavaria, Carl Krister of Silesia, Max Emanuel of Bavaria and Schmidt & Company of Austria were all successfully exporting, although none of these ever recovered its worldwide dominance after the ban on German wares during the First World War.

The availability of particular raw materials led to the factories producing distinctive hard-paste porcelain, which was grey and translucent and quite unlike British wares. The Merchandise Marks Act of 1887 banned unmarked imports, and pieces thereafter were made bearing circular printed marks 'Made in Germany' or 'Made in Austria' underneath. The Act was very unpopular with the foreign manufacturers. On 1st September 1889 *The Pottery Gazette* reported:

> The law respecting Trade Marks now in force in England, which is far more rigorous than the previous legislation on this subject, has caused considerable dissatisfaction in German industrial circles, its provisions being considered so stringent as to render the import of German articles into England very difficult. The law itself, according to German judgement, is not so objectionable as the severity with which it is applied.

There were no customs officers at the time, so imports would be checked by those in the trade. Any china marked 'Foreign' was not acceptable as the country of origin had to be specified. After the First World War German companies sent their wares first to Czechoslovakia or Austria, where the pieces were marked for export, so that they would not appear to originate in Germany, which was very unpopular with the buying public. As a newly created state, Czechoslovakia was tolerated by the British. Unmarked wares did, however, still slip through. (In the United States of America the McKinley Tariff Act of 1891 required the same declaration of origin and also imposed tariffs on imports, beginning their protectionist policy.) As well as all these obstacles being put in their way, German manufacturers met with resistance from anti-German British retailers. Still they persevered and tried a variety of decorations in relief with heavy gold and gaudy enamel embellishments. Some factories began producing gaily coloured and lustre ware instead of the sober white, bright pink being the most popular colour. Max Emanuel & Company of Mitterteich, Bavaria, produced the best. As soon as peace had been signed in 1918 German imports resumed, with firms supplying cheaper and better-value ware than ever

A coloured cat in boot with the arms of Bexhill-on-Sea, by Gemma.

BEXHILL ON SEA

before. The British potters could never understand how the Germans could produce such presentable goods at such reasonable prices from so far a distance. It may have been due to the cheaper ceramic body and cheap labour (sometimes prison inmates and prisoners of war). They produced cheaper pieces for export so as not to compete with their own internal market.

Pieces marked 'Gemma' were made by Schmidt & Company of Carlsbad, Bohemia. After the war they were also marked 'Czechoslovakia' because they were exported via the newly formed state. Gemma ware comprises a wide array of original shapes; particularly good were the puzzle range of jugs, cups, watering cans and teapots. They also include some pretty green–yellow pieces with transfer views that seemed to wrap themselves around the shapes.

Max Emanuel made a large range of bathing beauties, flappers and other figures, such as a bell-hop with a suitcase and a child riding a donkey, all lemon/rust coloured or lustre, some with lucky white heather instead of a crest. These had impressed four-digit stock numbers (five-digit items were much later). These numbers were usually accompanied by the impressed word 'Foreign' or 'Germany'. Some of these items are brightly coloured.

Saxony china was produced by Wilhelm Kutzscher & Company of Schwarzenberg, Saxony, and their wares have a distinctive white porcelain. They made a varied range, including a hot-air balloon with basket, and a steam locomotive inscribed 'R. H. and D. R.' (Romney Hythe and Dymchurch Railway). They produced an interesting range of cats with painted features, in active poses such as singing while holding sheet music.

The German manufacturers covered a vast range but never really matched the quality of the British makers.

Popular collecting themes

Coloured cottages

Two potteries excelled at coloured cottages – W. H. Goss and Willow Art. The models were made in the same way but mostly left unglazed. It was Adolphus Goss who, in 1893, first introduced a range of coloured cottages copied from historic buildings. The first seven were nightlights and some examples found today still have traces of candle wax inside. The smoke came out of hollow chimneys and the windows were moulded with extra thin porcelain to let the light shine out when a candle was placed in the open section at the back. The demand for the nightlights was such that Adolphus extended the range with smaller houses, visiting chosen landmarks and measuring, sketching and photographing to get an exact likeness in porcelain. There are forty-two different Goss cottages in total, some with variations in the moulding, such as Charles Dickens's House at Gads Hill; this was first produced with ivy on each side of the front door but when the ivy was trimmed back on the real house to reveal two side windows the Goss factory remoulded its model to include the windows. Willow Art produced thirty-five coloured houses; some, like Shakespeare's House and Ann Hathaway's Cottage, were made in great numbers and various sizes; others, like the Dick Whittington Inn near Stourbridge, had few examples made. The attention to detail was legendary with most of the manufacturers. Grafton cottages were usually delicately glazed. Edwin Leadbeater of Willow Art had earlier worked for Robinson & Leadbeater, and in 1919 started up Leadbeater Art on £300 capital. In 1920 a report in *The Pottery Gazette* praised the speed

Goss cottages: Charles Dickens's House at Gads Hill, Rochester, and Ann Hathaway's Cottage at Shottery, near Stratford-upon-Avon.

Willow Art's Dick Whittington Inn near Stourbridge, with the history of the inn printed on the reverse.

with which a new model could be produced:

> Apart from the tiny miniatures which used to be popular selling lines at 6¹/2d, Mr Leadbeater is bringing out models of monuments, notable buildings etc., for souvenir and commemorative purposes. These are quaintly tinted up by hand, very often quite realistically, although they are always very moderate in price. It is surprising how quickly, with enterprising zeal, some of these new models can be produced. A little time ago Mr Leadbeater was asked by a big buyer to copy a model for a seasonal trade. Within 10 days the first sample was in the buyer's hands and the latter was prompted to admit that it reminded him of how German manufacturers of such wares used to handle their enquiries in the years before the war.

Old Church, Bonchurch, Isle of Wight, by Leadbeater Art, and John Knox's House at Edinburgh, by Willow Art.

German potteries had been supplying the British market with bisque cottages, often as nightlights and usually unglazed. They lacked detail and were not exact reproductions of original cottages. An exception to this is the 'Ladies of Llangollen' and 'Fairmaid's House, Perth' cottages. Max Emanuel & Company of Mitterteich, Bavaria, made Mosanic china, exporting a wide range of unglazed stone-coloured buildings to Britain, although they were not made in huge quantities. They were usually marked with six-figure numbers pressed out on the base.

Named models

Goss led the field with its clearly labelled artefacts found in museums and churches across Britain and elsewhere. The *Goss Record*, which was first published in 1900 by a collector named J. J. Jarvis, was a catalogue of agents' names and addresses, plus a detailed listing of all the latest named models brought out by W. H. Goss. The booklet had no official connection with the Goss factory but was certainly helpful to its army of collectors. It was updated until 1921 and is the best way we have of establishing the date a model was brought out apart from the registration mark. Many Goss models were made in several sizes, the large ones being very large. For example, the Aberdeen Bronze Pot was made in three sizes: small (63 mm high), medium (89 mm high) and large (133 mm high, with multiple crests).

Most other potteries made their own versions of named models. Carlton, Grafton and Shelley carefully labelled their

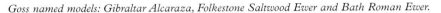

Goss named models: Gibraltar Alcaraza, Folkestone Saltwood Ewer and Bath Roman Ewer.

artefacts with as much historical information as would fit on the base or back, as well as faithfully numbering them to assist collectors. Some even had lids, such as the Jersey Milk Can, number 242, by Carlton. Carlton appears to have ceased making these named and numbered models by 1914.

Most factories made numerous vases, jugs and ewers and left them unnamed. They were the cheapest type of crested souvenir – simply vessels to carry a coat of arms. Multi-crested pots included a three-handled loving cup. There were far more unnamed models made than named models, and these appeal today to most collectors, who collect for the crest rather than the shape.

Animals

Arcadian and other factories produced innovative ranges of animals, realistic and comical and even grotesque! Sales of animals and related shapes (such as dog kennels or animals perched on hat boxes, armchairs and ashtrays) eventually exceeded those of the more sober Goss shapes, whereupon Goss belatedly made its own range of animals, which were of exceptional quality. Huntley Goss was running the firm at this time and his two sons designed the animals; Richard John Goss in particular made the dog, hippopotamus, rhinoceros and lions. Some of these were displayed for the first time at the British Empire Exhibition of 1924–5. After 1929 the animals were no

A comical Woody Woodpecker by Carlton, with the arms of Northampton.

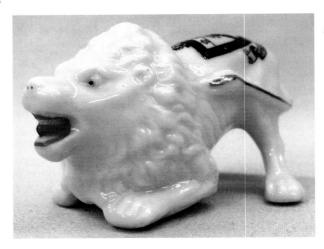

Willow Art's roaring lion, with the arms of Leamington Spa.

longer made, but the Third Period range of 1929–39, brought out under Harold Robinson, comprised a selection of tiny Arcadian and Willow Art animals marked with 'Goss England'. The Goss mark ensures they fetch five to six times the price for identical shapes marked with another pottery's mark.

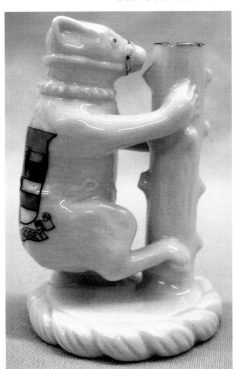

The widest and most interesting animal ranges came from Arcadian, Carlton and Grafton. Arcadian produced a realistic range of cats, dogs, rabbits, fish and farmyard animals and birds. Most factories favoured the pig, in all sorts of poses, as it was the Edwardian symbol of good luck. Gemma even modelled them as court figures, including a judge in a wig and a prisoner with padlock. Birds were also favourites, from wise owls winking and pelicans labelled 'A wonderful bird is the pelican, his beak will hold more than his belican', to more serious studies of geese, ducks, turkeys, parrots and wild birds. Many of the animals were historic, such as the bear and ragged staff from Warwick, Bill Sykes's Bulldog, the Wembley Lion and the ubiquitous grinning Cheshire Cat, taken from Lewis Carroll's novel *Alice in Wonderland* (1865). Animals from the regions include the Manx Cat with no tail and the rare

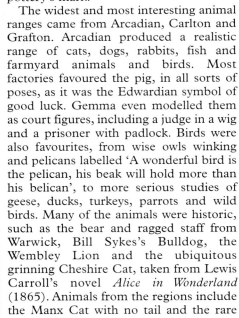

A bear and ragged staff from Warwick, by Grafton.

Carlton boar's head mustard pot and lid wearing the spiked helmet of the Emperor Wilhelm II of Prussia (note the long moustache!) in a piece that is doubly insulting to the Emperor.

three-legged Manx Dog, the Scottish Terrier, Highland Bull, Shetland Pony, Welsh Goat (inscribed *Yr Afr Cymreig*), Hampshire Hog, Jersey Cow and Staffordshire Bulldog. Birds include the Royston Crow, Norwich Canary, Manx Warbler and Aylesbury Duck. Among the exotic animals produced are crocodiles, camels, rhinoceroses, bears, seals, hippopotami, lions, monkeys, elephants, cougars and even kangaroos.

The First World War at sea

War models were produced soon after the commencement of hostilities in 1914. Today they provide us with a fascinating potted history of the First World War. In 1914 the Royal Navy had nearly twice as many battleships as the German navy. Several factories produced a fleet of British ships, including HMS *Iron Duke*, HMS *Tiger*, HMS *Renown*, HMS *Australia* and HMS *Canada*. The most realistic were by Carlton and Savoy. Grafton, Shelley and Willow Art produced a few ships, of which HMS *Lion* was one. To the public the dreadnoughts seemed invincible and bolstered the feeling of British sea power.

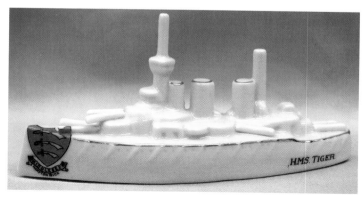

HMS 'Tiger' by Carlton, with the arms of Hampton Wick, Middlesex.

*HMS 'Renown'
by Carlton, with
the arms of
Kendal.*

A disastrous attack by a German U-boat on Cunard's RMS *Lusitania* on 7th May 1915 left over a thousand passengers dead. It had been bound for Liverpool from New York. The worldwide reaction to this sinking provoked considerable anti-German feeling, especially in the United States, which entered the war two years later. Carlton produced a magnificent model of the four-funnelled *Lusitania*, its fate printed on the side. The firm also made the two-funnelled HMHS *Anglia*, a hospital ship, bearing a large red cross on the side, as a pair with the *Lusitania*. The *Anglia* was produced in 1917, after it had been sunk by a mine in the English Channel in November 1915. Another rare model by Carlton is a half-submerged submarine.

*A Carlton battleship with
the arms of Liverpool,
and a rare Shelley
'Aquitania', with the
arms of Gourock.*

Three yachts: (left) a foreign example with billowing sail; (centre) a Gemma yacht with an anchor on the side; (right) a Shelley yacht in full sail.

Left: *A rare 'Model of Torpedo Boat Destroyer' by Savoy.*

Carlton's submarine 'E.9.', Swan China's bust of a sailor 'HMS Dreadnought, the Handy Man', Willow Art's kitbag and Arcadian's sailor winding a capstan.

The Earl Kitchener naval memorial at Marwick Head, Orkney, by Arcadian (dated 1916).

Civilian vessels, including trawlers, were requisitioned for war service. In 1914 Willow Art produced a liner that had been converted to a troop carrier. Trawlers became minesweepers, such as the HMMS *Gowan Lea*. Arcadian and Savoy both produced torpedo boat destroyers, the Savoy models being particularly delicate. There were a few naval figures made and these include various sailors, such as the Arcadian seaman winding a capstan, and busts with tilted hats labelled 'HMS *Queen Elizabeth*' or 'HMS *Dreadnought*'. Grafton produced a lifebelt with a German officer's head inside. They also made a seated sailor holding a model submarine, sometimes found inscribed 'We've got "U" well in hand'. Busts of Admirals Beatty and Jellicoe (as well as of Field Marshals Roberts and Kitchener) were made, and all manner of naval guns, torpedoes, mines and capstans. A rare piece is the 'Earl Kitchener Memorial' to commemorate his drowning off Marwick Head, Orkney, on 5th June 1916 on HMS *Hampshire*. Even the Scarborough lighthouse was modelled, complete with shell holes; this had been damaged in the bombardment by German warships on 16th December 1914.

The First World War on land

The grim reality of life in the trenches was a world away from the patriotic china figures of Tommy in action – in bayonet attack, using a machine gun or throwing a hand grenade. Bruce Bairnsfather's cartoon character Old Bill featured in a series of comical situations on porcelain. The china producers

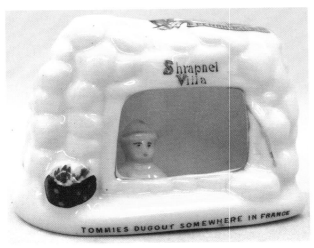

Carlton's 'Shrapnel Villa' – 'Tommies Dugout somewhere in France', with a character reputed to be Old Bill peeping out.

Grafton's Mills hand grenade with metal pin, Grafton's desert gun, Shelley's howitzer and Carlton's machine gun with solid stand.

sentimentalised the war. Homely fireplaces labelled 'Wait till the boys come home' were placed in homes as sources of comfort. The weapons of war were glamorised with crested china models of machine guns, howitzers, field guns, desert guns, trench mortars, guns on sleds and even guns on the backs of vehicles, labelled 'Anti-aircraft motors'. Shells and bullets were also portrayed in porcelain. Carlton made a triangular-based machine gun with hollow and solid base, and Savoy a two-piece machine gun on a tripod with a gun that swivelled round on the base; this is now a rare piece. In 1916 Arcadian registered the

Carlton's 'Map of Blighty', Swan China's Tommies' hut and Arcadian's despatch rider.

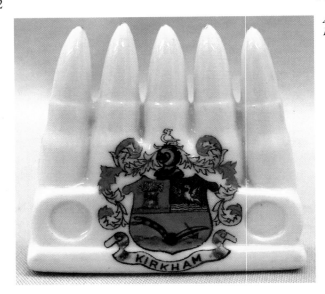

A clip of bullets, with the arms of Kirkham, by Arcadian.

canister bomb, German stick grenade, hairbrush grenade and German incendiary bomb.

Cars were also modelled. Savoy's armoured car was a modified Talbot with an open top and soldiers manning the guns. Shelley's was an enclosed Belgian armoured car with a small side door for entry. The Carlton Royal Naval Air Service riveted car was a highly modified 1917 Lancia.

The first tank was christened 'Little Willie', the next 'Big Willie', and then came the giant, heavy HMLS (His Majesty's Land Ship) *Mother*. After that, the Mark I had trailing wheels and was copied by Savoy, Arcadian, Grafton and Willow Art. Marks II and III followed. Carlton made a Vickers Mark II tank in 1922. Arcadian modelled the Whippet tank in 1918 with its large hexagonal gun turret at the rear, a large and scarce model. Several factories produced a wheelless Mark IV tank. Carlton and

Arcadian's sandbag, with the arms of Stamford.

Grafton's Whippet tank, with the arms of Brighton.

Below: *Carlton's HMLS money box Mark IV tank and Savoy's 'HMS Donner Blitzen' with long guns and side turrets.*

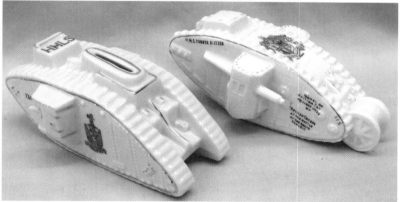

Grafton labelled theirs 'HMLS *Crème-de-Menthe*' after the name of the leading tank in the attack on Courcelette in 1916. Tanks numbered 130 on the side commemorate the fund-raising efforts of the 'Tank Bank' at various London landmarks and suburbs in the winter of 1917–18. This huge tank helped raise vital funds for the war effort. The enormous Arcadian Mark IV tank, sometimes painted a garish lustre or in camouflage colours, was made for shop display. Tank banks with slots for money were not very practical. As the only way to retrieve the contents was to smash the tank they are consequently now rare. The Savoy Mark IV tank is numbered 515 on the side; this was a 'female' tank, armed with machine guns only. The Renault FT17 light tank was the standard tank of the French army for two decades after the war. Corona and Grafton made a model of this; Carlton's is incorrectly named a 'Whippet' tank. Carlton also copied the only Italian Fiat tank design.

A Red Cross van and armoured car with Rolls-Royce front, both by Carlton.

Other First World War vehicles made by Carlton are the RNAS anti-aircraft motor, the Rolls-Royce armoured car and an ambulance with three red crosses on the sides. Around twenty other souvenir potteries made an ambulance or Red Cross van. The Arcadian, Wembley and Botolph Red Cross vans are Model T Fords with the distinctive flat top. Savoy made a long ambulance called an Argyll, and the curtained example by Grafton has an inscription underneath explaining it is a motor ambulance car given to the Staffordshire China Operatives. Various coloured crosses in red or blue and inscriptions mentioning the British Red Cross or the St John's Ambulance Association make this a detailed, well-crafted model.

Shelley's Mark I tank, Carlton's motorcyclist with sidecar and Savoy's Argyll Red Cross van.

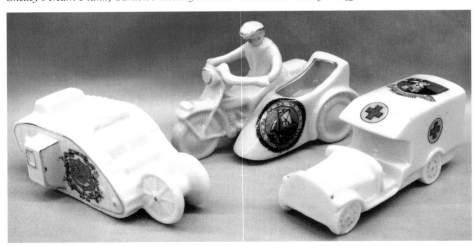

Above: *A Savoy French trench helmet inscribed on the reverse 'Worn by the Dauntless French Poilu', with the arms of Carnforth.*

Right: *A bell tent with open flaps, with the arms of the City of Peterborough, by Savoy.*

First World War hats include forage and peaked caps, glengarries, German spiked helmets, Balmoral bonnets, French trench helmets, steel helmets and Royal Flying Corps caps. Grafton modelled the impossibly balanced boot with puttees, and various manufacturers made kitbags, water bottles, folded telescopes, trench lamps, Gurkha knives and revolvers, even drums and bugles.

Leadbeater Art war memorials made after November 1918: Cumberland and Westmorland, and Harrogate.

At the end of the war the manufacturers added inscriptions to their war pieces, particularly the tanks: 'The Victory of Justice, Armistice of the Great War, signed Nov. 11th 1918'.

The First World War in the air

By 1914 Germany had advanced its airship design, mainly owing to Count Ferdinand von Zeppelin. Zeppelins, as they became known, were filled with inflammable hydrogen and were used by the Germans to bomb northern France and Belgium. In 1915 two Zeppelin bombs were successfully dropped on Britain, over Great Yarmouth and Sheringham. There were over forty more raids like this but, surprisingly, the crested china Zeppelins sold very well. Arcadian tactlessly registered its German airship six days after Germany's worst raid on Britain and other manufacturers followed. The Shelley model was the most like the L33 produced in 1917.

The first British airship was the Beta of 1909, copied by Willow Art and clearly showing the suspension wires. This observation balloon was superseded by the Drachen kite observer sausage balloon, copied by Arcadian, also with detailed wires. This model was made semi-inflated, perhaps from a photograph in a newspaper. Carlton made a Zeppelin with a black Maltese cross pressed out on the side, sometimes with French air force or RAF roundels on one end. After 1918 the cross was left unpainted.

An Arcadian observer sausage balloon, half-inflated, with the arms of Pontardulais.

A Zeppelin with French roundels, with the crest of the City of London, by Carlton China.

A British airship with a suspended engine by Arcadian, with the crest of Cardinal Wolsey.

Carlton's monoplane with moveable propeller, Shelley's Bury St Edmunds German Zeppelin bomb, Shelley's biplane and Blériot warplane.

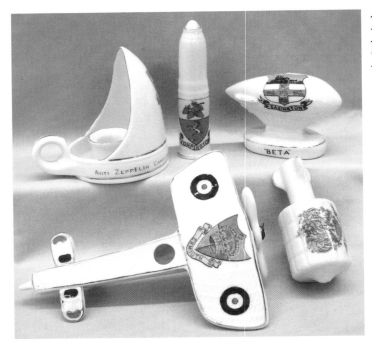

A Shelley anti-Zeppelin candlestick, Arcadian's anti-aircraft shell, a Willow Art Beta airship, a Willow Art monoplane with RAF roundels on the wings and striped tail fins, and an Arcadian German aerial torpedo.

Arcadian made a British Sea Scout airship with its distinctive observation platform, known as a 'Blimp', which was developed to escort ships and help alert them to the presence of submarines. Arcadian registered the model in December 1916, a year after the more common airship. Savoy copied the SL11 that came down in Cuffley, Hertfordshire, in 1916.

Models were also made of the bombs dropped by the Zeppelins, such as the 1915 Sheringham bomb with its three-bladed propeller. Most factories made a Goldschmidt incendiary bomb, which had fallen on Bury St Edmunds. A percussion cap underneath exploded on impact. Goss made a similar bomb based on one dropped from a German Zeppelin on Maldon in 1915. Registered in 1916, when Arcadian began production of various bombs and grenades, the Cooper bomb, with its distinctive four legs, was named 'British Aerial Bomb'. This was a bomb dropped from the warplanes.

The other early aviation invention was the cloth and plywood biplane. Initially these were used for reconnaissance but their full military potential was soon realised and the Blériot was developed to carry bombs. Military flying was controlled by the Royal Flying Corps and the Royal Naval Air Service. Several potteries made monoplanes and biplanes from as early as 1912, and in 1915, a year into the war, some applied coloured roundels (red outside for French, blue for British) as an aid to

Willow Art's airman's cap, with the arms of Farnborough.

Right: *A Carlton British searchlight, sometimes named 'The Zeppelin Finder', with the arms of Oban.*

identification. Willow Art and Goss sold RFC and RNAS badges on a variety of shapes; after April 1918, when the RFC and RNAS combined to form the Royal Air Force, they made RAF badges too. Early war aeroplanes were mainly biplanes. Savoy and Carlton made magnificent models with and without solid struts, coloured roundels, tail fins and moveable propellers. The Carlton model could be a Sopwith 1½ strutter. Arcadian's and Grafton's versions were less intricate. The Arcadian model was introduced in December 1916 and resembled the Sopwith Scout plane, which was used by the RFC after September 1916. The BE2c biplane was copied by Grafton China. Shelley made a version which was very like a Sopwith Camel. The Shelley monoplane is labelled 'Model of a Blériot Warplane' and has a fixed propeller. Carlton's, Savoy's and Arcadian's V-winged models are rather delicately moulded; after 1912 Arcadian included a circular shape in the middle to carry the crest. It can also be found with various sorts of propeller: with two or three blades, revolving or fixed. The more common Arcadian and Willow Art monoplanes appeared after 1912. The small German planes with pilots were made after the war. Willow Art made large aeroplane propellers, often with RFC, RNAS and RAF badges.

Grafton made a unique model of an airfield tractor with a driver. This was a Holt army tractor used for towing aeroplanes. Shelley produced the best anti-Zeppelin candlestick, named and correctly moulded. The Arcadian version has the handle in the wrong position and does not block the light of the candle. Carlton made the detailed British searchlight, 'The Zeppelin Finder'.

Swan China produced the bust of an airman named 'Arry, and Willow Art two versions of a standing airman, one holding a medal, the other with arms straight. Savoy, Willow Art and Aynsley made an airman's cap; the Savoy one is particularly detailed, with the RFC badge in relief.

50

A Norfolk Crest China cricket cap, a Florentine cricket bag and an Arcadian cricket bat.

Tips for collectors and makers' marks

Crested china can be found in most antique shops. Antiques and collectors' fairs and car-boot sales all over Britain, usually at weekends and bank holidays, are worth attending because one never knows what might turn up. Auction houses, the Internet and specialist dealers with mail-order sales lists are the best places to turn to as they tend to be more reliable about the condition of a piece.

Before purchasing, check the condition of a piece. Pay the full price only if it is perfect. Slightly damaged pieces can be restored but they will never be worth the price of a perfect item. When buying by mail order make sure you can return the goods for a full refund if you are not happy with them. Any item with a faded crest, crack or chip is damaged. Goss collectors consider a piece with rubbed gilding as substandard. However, the other makes of china are not devalued by rubbed gilding – many of them were made with poor gilding, if any, to start with. Firing flaws are common with this ware and only very bad manufacturing flaws will reduce the value of an item. There exists some poorly made, crude china that is also decorated with coats of arms. These items – usually heavy, cumbersome ornamental or table ware – should not be confused with the high-quality, translucent, delicate crested ware. Remember the translucency: there are some very fine shapes that are almost see-through. A good guide is to buy only what you find visually appealing.

Having a target theme to keep to can limit your expenditure. Be careful not to tell all the dealers you come across what you are looking for as you could find they bid up the cost of suitable pieces at auction because they are all bidding against each other on your behalf! Choose a dealer you like and let him or her alone help you find the models you need.

Do not pay more than you feel something is worth, however much you desire it. Above all, enjoy your collecting. Join the band of collectors who use their skills and knowledge to build up a collection of value!

Identifying W. H. Goss china

Most Goss china is marked with a factory stamp. Only some pre-1860 pieces, including halves of pairs of figurines, were not marked (unless they were the few pieces that managed to slip out by the back door). Impressed marks were applied when the parian was still damp and fresh out of the mould. Early (pre-1916) pieces were marked in this way. Versions of the more usual black Gosshawk printed mark were used from 1862 to 1934 on heraldic ware. Most Goss ware has a coloured squiggle on the base. This is the paintress's individual signature mark, using the last colour of enamel she happened to have on her brush. Faulty workmanship could be traced back because of the personal mark, and three warnings meant dismissal. The Goss standards were high and no badly painted crests were tolerated. Faulty

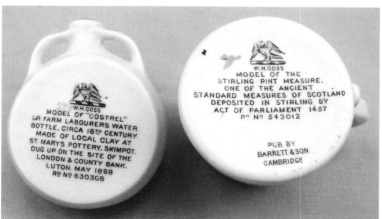

The undersides of two Goss models. The coloured marks are the paintresses' marks. The agency mark on the Stirling pint measure (right) shows it was made to order for the Cambridge agent.

goods were dumped on the spoil heap at the back of the factory. Until the 1970s this was a large mound but it has since been excavated by keen collectors on numerous occasions. The gilded mark on the base was the gilder's mark; the same strict rules applied to the gilding as to the enamelling.

Identifying other manufacturers

The other major firms also had about five or six variations to their factory mark. However, almost half of all crested china has no factory mark at all, probably more because of carelessness by the staff than any deliberate policy. Certain potteries numbered their ware and these numbers have been recorded in the *Price Guide to Crested China* by Nicholas Pine. Shelley, Carlton, Grafton, Savoy and Willow Art all used numbering on some of their products.

The main manufacturers' marks are illustrated below.

Glossary

Bats: portable perforated iron shelves used to support ware in the kiln.

Biscuit: pottery that has been fired once but not yet glazed.

Clammins: the large door of the oven that is bricked up for firing and broken down when the contents are removed (drawing).

Coat of arms: heraldic device used to decorate the china.

Crest: general term for coat of arms (technically it is the top part of the coat of arms).

Dipping: briefly immersing china in a tub of glaze.

Earthenware: ceramic ware with a main ingredient of ball clay, which makes it plastic and possible to fashion by hand before firing. When glazed it is impervious.

Enamel: a chemical colour that is painted on to the glaze and then fired in a muffle kiln.

Fettle: to smooth down the rough edges of casts and seams in green ware, where hollow halves have been joined together to make a whole piece.

Fireman: craftsman trained to organise and supervise the firings of his bottle oven.

Firing: heating to a certain temperature in an oven in order to turn moist clay into hard ware.

Flues: channels below the oven floor which spread the heat.

Gilding: edging with gold, using a fine paintbrush.

Glaze: hard, thin, glassy permanent film applied to the surface of the porcelain, rendering it impervious.

Glost kiln: small oven for firing freshly glazed ware.

Green ware: unfired ware just out of the moulds.

Hollow ware: hollow shapes.

Kaolin: white china clay, consisting of alumina (39.77 per cent), silica (46.33 per cent) and water (13.9 per cent).

Kiln: oven for firing ceramic ware.

Mould: casing, usually made of plaster of Paris, for coating parian or pressing earthenware.

Muffle kiln: small oven for firing enamelled and gilded ware.

Parian: a type of porcelain, named after Paros, an island in the Aegean Sea famed for its marble quarries.

Porcelain: fine earthenware; white, ivory or pale grey, translucent and vitreous.

Potbank: pottery factory.

Pottery: general term for clay wares or the factory where it is made.

Print: transfer decoration on tissue made from an engraved copper plate spread with ink.

Props or cones: supports made of fine silica sand to keep pieces apart during firing.

Saggars: fireclay containers for holding ware during the biscuit and glost firing.

Slip: liquid parian mixture.

Terracotta: very heavy unglazed earthenware, dark reddish brown in colour.

Wareboards: large wooden boards for carrying ware about the factory, usually on one shoulder.

Further reading

Jarvis, J. J. (editor). *The Goss Record 8th and War Editions*. Milestone Publications, 1989 (reprinted from 1914 edition).

Owen, Frank. *The New Goss Record*. Six Penny Pig, 1993.

Pine, Lynda. *Goss and Crested China: A Collector's Guide*. Miller's Publications, 2001.

Pine, Lynda (editor). *Goss & Crested China* (illustrated monthly sales catalogue of heraldic china). Milestone Publications (email: lynda.pine@btconnect.com).

Pine, Lynda and Nicholas. *William Henry Goss: The Story of the Staffordshire Family of Potters Who Invented Heraldic Porcelain*. Milestone Publications, 1987.

Pine, Nicholas. *The Price Guide to Arms and Decorations on Goss China*. Milestone Publications, 1991. The only book on the crests, valuable for its listings and information.

Pine, Nicholas. *The Concise Encyclopaedia and 2000 Price Guide to Goss China*. Milestone Publications, 2000.

Pine, Nicholas. *2000 Price Guide to Crested China*. Milestone Publications.

Seabrook, Maggie and Sam. *Collecting Miniature Coloured Cottages*. New Cavendish Books, 1996.

(The books listed above are all available from Lynda Pine at The Goss & Crested China Club, 62 Murray Road, Horndean, Hampshire PO8 9JL. Telephone: 023 9259 7440. Website: www.gosscrestedchina.co.uk E-mail: info@gosschinaclub.co.uk)

The Goss Hawk: the monthly magazine of the Goss Collectors' Club. Email: editor@gosscollectorsclub.org

A Boer War pith helmet with the badge of the Royal Garrison Artillery, by Aynsley.

Places to visit

The Goss & Crested China Club and Museum, 62 Murray Road, Horndean, Hampshire PO8 9JL. Telephone: 023 9259 7440. Website: www.gosschinaclub.co.uk E-mail: info@gosschinaclub.co.uk Free entry to museum. Large Victorian-style showroom, full range of stock. Send two first-class stamps to receive free 'Introduction to Collecting' pack, latest sales catalogue and book list.

The Potteries Museum and Art Gallery, Bethesda Street, Hanley, Stoke-on-Trent ST1 3DE. Telephone: 01782 232323. Website: www.stoke.gov.uk/museums

Where to buy and sell

Peter Bolton, EPK Collectables. Telephone: 01702 205002. E-mail: crested@epkcollectables@tiscali.co.uk

Lynda Pine, 62 Murray Road, Horndean, Hampshire PO8 9JL. Telephone: 023 9259 7440. Website: www.gosschinaclub.co.uk E-mail: info@gosschinaclub.co.uk and lynda.pine@btconnect.com

David Taylor, Crested China Company, Highfield, Windmill Hill, Driffield, East Yorkshire YO25 5EF. Telephone: 0870 300 1300.
Website: www.thecrestedchinacompany.com

REGISTRATION CHART FOR DATING CRESTED CHINA

For example, a Hornsea Atwick Vase bears the registration number 500864. If you look at the chart, you can see that it was first registered between 1907 and 1908. It would have been made for a number of years after that date.

Year	Rd. No.	Year	Rd. No.	Year	Rd. No.	Year	Rd. No.
1884	1	1897	291241	1910	552000	1923	694999
1885	19754	1898	311658	1911	574817	1924	702671
1886	40480	1899	331707	1912	594195	1925	710165
1887	64520	1900	351202	1913	612431	1926	718057
1888	90483	1901	368154	1914	630190	1927	726330
1889	116648	1902	385088	1915	644935	1938	734370
1890	141273	1903	402913	1916	653521	1929	742725
1891	163767	1904	425017	1917	658988	1930	751160
1892	185713	1905	447548	1918	662872	1931	760580
1893	205240	1906	471486	1919	666128	1932	769670
1894	224720	1907	493487	1920	673750	1933	779292
1895	246975	1908	518415	1921	680147	1934	789018
1896	268392	1909	534963	1922	687144	1935	799097

Index